I0009032

HACKING ANALYSIS

AND

PROTECTION

Xenophon Koumourou

Table of Contents

Table of Figures

Abstract

Anybody that is using a computer, from home user to professional IT expert, once connected to the Internet, becomes automatically a hacker's potential target. In this book various attacking tools and methods commonly used by the attackers, to compromise your computer or network are being described and analyzed. Finally some countermeasures are introduced in order to avoid being a victim of any kind of attacker. All the demonstrated further examples are run by the author of the book.

Chapter 1

Theoretical approach to Hacking

1.1 Enumeration Methods

The attacker is looking for signatures of resources that can be used in an attack. He/she is also trying to define the type of OS the machines are using. Transport protocols, routing protocols, services of network devices are all good source of information for an attacker [1].

1.2 Different Attacking Methods

The attacking methods that hackers usually employ can be methodically applied over a long period of time (let's say a week or a month), rather than a single burst that most people thing they act like. The very first steps they are using to do so will be explained extensively further in this book, such as discovering, port scanning and enumerating [2].

1.3 Different types of attackers

Physically we have some people acting behind this attacks, this people can be categorized as persistent and casual attackers [2].

Persistent attacker

Persistent attacker can be described as a person who is well motivated for the actions he is performing. In simple words he has set a target for example, to break into a bank system and he is willing to spend as much time as it would require doing so.

Casual attacker

Casual attackers are looking for easy targets - to compromise systems that require less effort than systems persistent attackers would penetrate. They are after systems that can be compromised with little skills, though sometimes can be very sophisticated.

A common measure used to prevent attack is turning the power down on the wireless access point (AP). By turning the power down, the range of the AP signal is reduced. While this might stop the casual attacker, it won't stop a determined one. An attacker can boost his own signal and use an antenna to connect to the lower power AP [3].

1.4 Motivations for the attackers

There are many different reasons that encourage attackers to try and break into a system.

Notoriety: Is a main reason, as many of them would like to get famous.

Vigilantism: People sometimes can't sleep and they do not have better way to spend their time.

Challenge and Curiosity: Being able to compromise another system and use it for your own purposes is quite challenging especially for young people.

Financial gain: To top up your bank account by the use of your computer is not a bad idea.

Political and religious: Some people from one country attack web pages of another country because of a fanatic behavior.

Terrorism: This the new way to conduct terrorism attacks. Terrorists are getting modernized using the technology to create problems for people or countries which they hate.

Organized crime: Many people are meeting together with a common target, with methodical movements and strategy in order to archive their target.

Corporate Espionage: Staff of a company is getting information about their enemies company through their web site.

Disgruntled Employees: Employees who are not satisfied and they try to harm the company.

1.5 Methodologies

Discovery and reconnaissance: In this stage the attacker is actually collecting information about the target network is going to try and break into.

Scanning: Finding legitimate host or routers, physical devices that have IP addresses on the target networks.

Enumeration: Looking for services, users, shares and different resources that can become entry points on the target systems.

Penetration: Using the information, services and operating systems weaknesses in order to gain control. This is when the exploits really turn into reality.

Elevation: In this stage the attacker injects its current low level privileges into administrator in order to execute all the malicious codes he wants to use.

Pilfer: Pilfer is a concept which stands for illegally obtaining information, modifying it or observing it.

Expansion: It is when we start expanding our attack beyond the system we have compromised on other systems of the network.

Housekeeping: On this stage the attacker is covering his tracks, on the compromise system and also creates backdoors for his next attacks in a later stage [4].

Chapter 2

Hacking demonstration

2.1 Categories of Hacking tools

Hacking tools are, generally speaking, programs run by a hacker in order to help him in a number of ways to gain control over a server or stand alone PC without its owners knowledge. All such tools have interfaces through which the hacker interacts with the program. Some of them have GUI interfaces, command line interfaces or both. This chapter demonstrates a variety of them. In general in this book any tool that can be used by an attacker in order to help him compromise any system is considered as a hacking tool [5].

2.1.1 Network Investigation tools

Approaching the target: In order to access somebody's belongings in nature you have to know where they physically are. For example you need the postcode and street number. In virtual world one will need the IP address of a machine in order to take down, corrupt or even hijack. There are several network investigation tools that can help us to find the IP address we are after. In this book the "**SAM SPADE**" is being chosen to demonstrate this ability.

Sam Spade

Sam Spade is a comprehensive network investigation tool that can be used to find information about the IP address, such as "who" the address is registered to and the route between one's computer and the computer at the remote IP address. Then the registration records for this IP address can be queried and the Internet Service Provider (ISP) who owns the IP address can be discovered (including the contact information) [6].

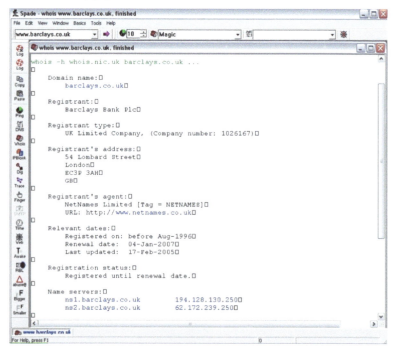

Figure 1: Sam Spade investigation tool

Bank hacking is a reality, it happens on a regular basis. Statistics that have been published [7] by security experts, say for instance that 96,000 attacks were launched from Brazil last year. As it can be seen in **Figure 1** when a potential attacker makes a simple "**whois**" query on a target bank's URL, in order to exploit it he gets the server names and also bank's servers IP addresses. At this point the system is wide open and vulnerable to malicious action.

2.1.2 LAN Scanners

Scanning tools are tools that explore another system, looking for vulnerabilities. While these can be used by security managers, wishing to fortify their security, the tools are as likely to be used by attackers to evaluate where to start an attack. In this chapter we can see a demonstration of some of these tools [8].

Nmap

Nmap is a very powerful utility as it supports many arguments and different interfaces it has for windows GUI and command line scriptable engine [9].

NMAP example

In the following example **Figure 2** there is the root command "**nmap**" then, the "**-sS**" parameter which stands for **S**tealth **S**ignatures and the **IP** address, that is chosen to be scanned. From the output of this command all the ports that are open can be viewed and the type of operating system the attacked machine is running, can be determined

C:\Documents and Settings\Xanthos\Desktop\dissertation tools\dissertation\nmap-3.93>

nmap –sS –PT –PI –O –T 3 82.45.194.21

Starting nmap 3.93 (http://www.insecure.org/nmap) at 2005-11-30 14:16 GMT Stan
dard Time
Insufficient responses for TCP sequencing (2), OS detection may be less accurate

Interesting ports on 82-45-194-21.stb.ubr02.hari.blueyonder.co.uk (82.45.194.21)
:
(The 1657 ports scanned but not shown below are in state: closed)
PORT   STATE   SERVICE
80/tcp   open   http
135/tcp filtered msrpc
137/tcp filtered netbios-ns
138/tcp filtered netbios-dgm
139/tcp filtered netbios-ssn
445/tcp filtered microsoft-ds
1025/tcp open   NFS-or-IIS
1026/tcp open   LSA-or-nterm
1214/tcp open   fasttrack
1434/tcp filtered ms-sql-m
5000/tcp open   UpnP
MAC Address: 00:11:1A:D2:30:01 (Motorola BCS)

Device type: general purpose

Running: Microsoft Windows 95/98/ME|NT/2K/XP

OS details: Microsoft Windows Millennium Edition (Me), Windows 2000 Professional

or Advanced Server, or Windows XP, Microsoft Windows 2000 Professional RC1 or Windows 2000 Advanced Server Beta3, Microsoft Windows 2000 Professional SP2, Microsoft Windows XP Pro SP1/SP2 or 2000 SP4

Nmap finished: 1 IP address (1 host up) scanned in 7.911 seconds

Figure 2: nmap example

Netcat

As it can be seen throughout this book, a plethora of network security and hacker tools are at our disposal. In most cases, each tool is used to focus on a specific goal. For example, some tools gather information about a network and its hosts. Others are used directly to exploit vulnerability. The most beneficial and well-used tools, however, are usually those that are multifunctional and appropriate for use in several different scenarios. Netcat is such a tool [10].

Netcat Example:

A single IP address was scanned "64.156.132.253" and the port range 20-80, as it can be concluded from the results in **Figure 3,** ports 22, 25 and 53 where open.

```
C:\netcat>nc –v –z 64.156.132.253 20-80

ns5.experts-exchange.com   [64.156.132.253]   53   (?)
open
ns5.experts-exchange.com   [64.156.132.253]   25   (?)
open
ns5.experts-exchange.com   [64.156.132.253]   22   (?)
open
```

Figure 3: netcat example

LANguard Network Scanner 2.0 .

LANguard Network Scanner is a Freeware security scanner for networks. It searches the network for hosts, shares and user names. Amongst many other functions it recognizes operating systems, as well as registry problems and tests password security. The scanner also provides comprehensive reports in HTML format on request. The LANguard Network Scanner is a comprehensive and easy-to-use tool [11].

LANguard example

In the following example a range of **IP** addresses are scanned "80.195.236.1-80.195.236.254". From the output of **LANguard** in **Figure 4** it can be observed that 46 hosts are alive. They all have at least 2 ports open and their OS are Windows and UNIX based systems.

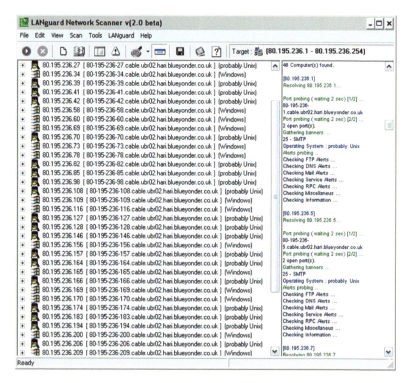

Figure 4: LANguard example

Softperfect Network Scanner

Softperfect Network Scanner is a multi-threaded IP, SNMP and NetBIOS scanner with a modern interface and several advanced features. It is intended for both system administrators and users who are interested in computer security. The program pings computers, scans for listening TCP ports and shows what types of resources are shared on a network (including system and hidden files). In addition, it allows the user to mount shared resources as network drives, browse them using Windows Explorer, filter the results list and more [12].

Softperfect example

Using **Softperfect Network Scanner** an IP range "80.195.236.1-80.195.236.254" was scanned. **Figure 5** shows that 44 hosts were alive and it can be noticed that it has successfully retrieved the MAC address of each host.

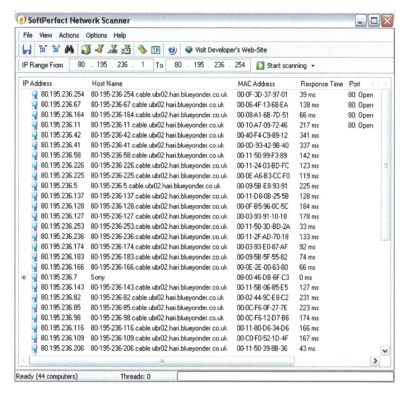

Figure 5: Softperfect Scanner

2.1.3 Wireless Scanners

As with LAN scanning tools, wireless scanning tools have now also become widely spread. While Wireless networking technology has now become popular, at the same time has introduced many security issues. Therefore wireless scanning tools are needed to check for any vulnerabilities at any wireless transmitter [13].

Network Stumbler

Network Stumbler is a tool for Windows that allows you to detect Wireless Local Area Networks (WLANs) using 802.11b, 802.11a and 802.11g. It has a number of useful features such as allowing to

- Verify that your network is set up the way you intended.

- Find locations with poor coverage in your WLAN.

- Detect other networks that might be causing interference with your network.

- Detect unauthorized "rogue" access points in your workplace.

- Help aim directional antennas for long-haul WLAN links.

- Use it recreationally for WarDriving [14].

Network Stumbler Example

Figure 6 below presents **Network Stumbler** which, through the wireless card scanning, has discovered 4 Access Points **AP**, where 3 of them **Figure 6** offer WEP encryption. **Figure 7** shows an **AP** with no security measures at all. Another important issue that can be noticed here is that all of the access points are broadcasting on the same 11 channel.

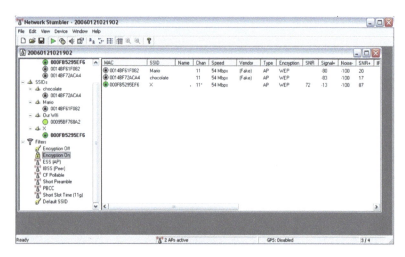

Figure 6: Network Stumbler AP with encryption

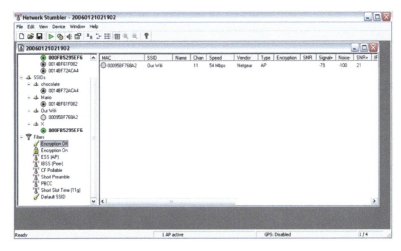

Figure 7: Network Stumbler AP without encryption

2.1.4 Protocol Analyzers

Protocol analyzer, analyses traffic across a network, packets can be observed according to their destination. A protocol analyzer will inform who or what is using up valuable network resources, when, where and why. It also captures conversations between two or more systems or devices. A sophisticated protocol analyzer will provide statistics and trend information on the captured traffic. Protocol analyzers provide information about the traffic flow on the LAN, from which device-specific information can be viewed [15].

Ethereal

Ethereal is a free Graphic User Interface (GUI) network protocol analyzer, it has several powerful features, including a rich display filter language and the ability to view the reconstructed stream of a TCP session [16].

Ethereal example:

In this scenario **Ethereal network protocol analyzer** was used at the same time that an **IPSCANNER** was running so the echo from the alive hosts in **Figure 8** can be viewed. By analyzing the highlighted acknowledgment packet the MAC address of the alive hosts can be obtained. In this example the host with the **IP address 80.195.236.171** is alive and his **MAC address is 00:12:3f:0b:31:1a**.

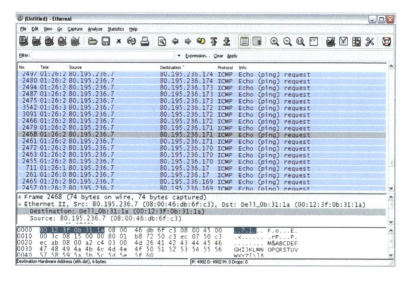

Figure 8: Ethereal network protocol analyzer

2.2 Common Gateway Interface (CGI)

The Common Gateway Interface (CGI) is a standard for interfacing external applications with information servers, such as HTTP or Web servers. A plain HTML document that the Web daemon retrieves is static, which means it exists in a constant state: a text file that does not change. A CGI program, on the other hand, is executed in real-time, so that it can output dynamic information. Some times though some CGI programs are badly written thus allowing some requests through, providing users with private information, such as /etc/passwd files.[17].

Vulnerabilities

Port 80 is the standard port for websites, and it can have a lot of different security issues.

These holes can allow an attacker to gain either administrative access to the website, or even the web server itself. CGI is a generic interface for calling external programs to crunch numbers, query databases, generate customized graphics, or perform any other server-side task [18].

Requests

"." ".." and "..."

These are the most common attack signatures in both web application exploitation and web server exploitation. It is used to allow an attacker or worm to change directories within your web server to gain access to sections that may not be public. Most CGI holes will contain some ".." requests.

Example:
http://www.amicotelecom.com/call2pk/index.php?p =../../../../../../etc/passwd

This shows an attacker requesting the web servers "system password file". If an attacker has the ability to browse outside the web server's root, then it may be possible to gather enough information to gain further privileges.

As we can see in this example **Figure 9,** vulnerability has been exploited to such an extent that it allows an attacker to view the **"/etc/passwd"** file through a normal web browser.

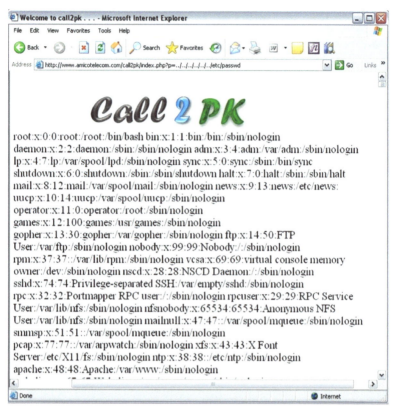

Figure 9: CGI exploitation

Cygwin
Linux-like environment for Windows

After retrieving the useful "/etc/passwd" file the attacker separates all the valid users in order to supply the password guessing tools. Here the whole process is presented.

Cygwin is a UNIX emulation that allows us to run some very useful UNIX commands under windows [19]. One of its very powerful commands is **awk** which is being used for this illustration. **Figure 10**.

Example of awk :

awk −F" " ' { for (i=1;i<=NF;i++) print $i }' root.txt | awk −F: ' {print $1} ' > users.txt

Explanation

awk: the command.

-F" " : the field separator which is the space (" ").

For (i=1;i<=NF;i++) print $i : with this loop we print all the fields which in this case we print all the users and their details one by one. For example: **root:x:0:0:root:/root:/bin/bash**.

root.txt: is being given here as **awk** input and it contains the servers **"\etc\passwd"** file.

| : pipeline command we pass this output as input to another **awk** command.

"–F:" : this time we set the ":" as the separator of the fields.

Print $1: Prints the 1st field of each line. In this case it prints all the valid users of this server.

>users.txt: the output goes into a text file called the users.txt in order to be used for a password guessing for all those users.

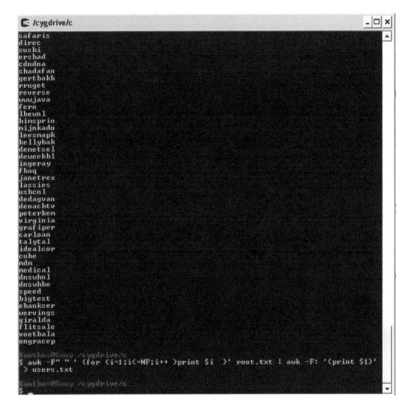

Figure 10: Cygwin usage for users separation

2.3 Password guessing tools

Password guessing tools: Once a valid IP address is being discovered, the family of authentication services been identified by a port scan and the "**\etc\passwd**" file containing all the valid usernames of the particular site is being retrieved, it's hard to resist an immediate password guess.

Brutus AET2

Brutus example: Using **Brutus password guessing tool** in **Figure 11** username file can be specified to be used as well as a word dictionary file to accomplish the password guessing [20].

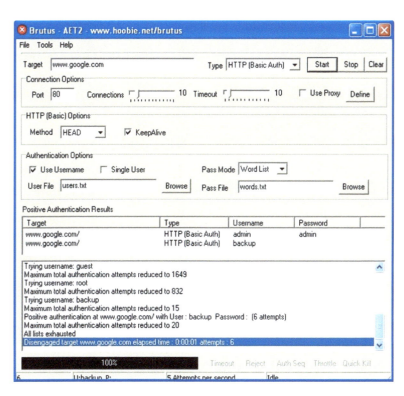

Figure 11: Brutus – AET2

WebCracker 4.0

WebCracker example:

Another powerful tool for password guessing is the WebCracker, as its demonstrated in **Figure 12 and Figure 13,** it tries up to 5000 combinations per minute [21].

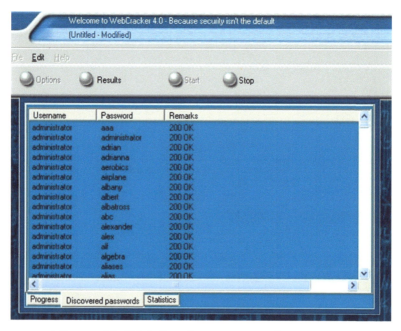

Figure 12: WebCracker password guessing

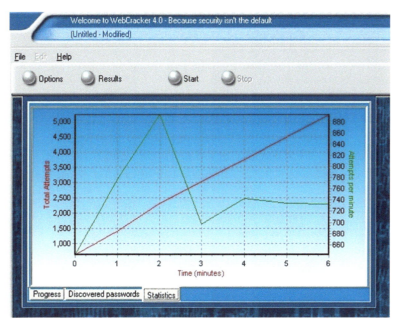

Figure 13: WebCracker statistics

@stake LC5

@stake LC5 is a very powerful tool which provides two critical capabilities to system administrators:

- LC5 helps administrators secure Windows and Unix-authenticated networks through comprehensive auditing of Windows NT, Windows 2000, Windows XP, and Unix user account passwords.
- LC5 recovers Windows and Unix user account passwords to streamline migration of users to another authentication system or to access accounts whose passwords are lost[22].

However, as with any other tool useful for administrators, **LC5** can help hackers discover the passwords on your local machines on your network once they have physical access to them.

The way it is done is by copying the
c:\windows\system32\config\SAM" file of windows
which stores all the passwords into hashes, and LC5
just turns those hashes into the passwords. In order to
copy the SAM file the hacker will need physical access
to the computer and load the machine with a bootable
CD. Windows will not allow copying the file or access it
while it is running [23]. An administrator though, once
he is logged into the computer, can install and run **LC5**
and get his employees' passwords from a local or
remote host on his network.

As we can see in **Figure 14**, @stake LC5 managed to
decrypt the password in **4s**, which is a very good result.

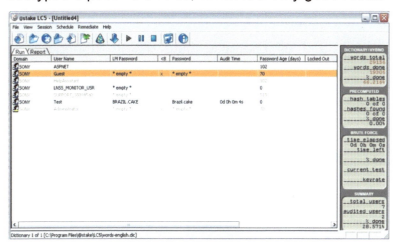

Figure 14: @stake LC5

The NTLM authentication protocol consists of two authentication protocols: the NT and the LM authentication protocol. These protocols use different hashing methods to securely store a user's password in the Windows security database (SAM or Active Directory-AD). As a consequence, the Windows security database contains an LM hash and an NT hash (also known as the Unicode hash) for every user account's password.

Compared with the NT hash-which takes much more time to break-the, LM hash is weak and easily cracked with brute-force attacks. Because of the way LM hashing works, the effective password length is limited to seven characters (even if the user's password is longer), and all characters are stored in uppercase characters (even if the password contains a combination of uppercase and lowercase characters).

2.4 Distributed Denial of Service (DDoS) attacks

Once the attacker, compromises one computer, following the above steps, its next step probably would be to expand beyond it, as **Figure 15** shows. The result of the expansion is causing a distributed, denial-of-service (DDoS) attack to a specific server. The flood of incoming messages to the target system (server) essentially forces it to shut down, thereby denying service to the systems legitimate users [24].

In reality there are many victims in a DDoS attack, the final target as well the systems controlled by the intruder.

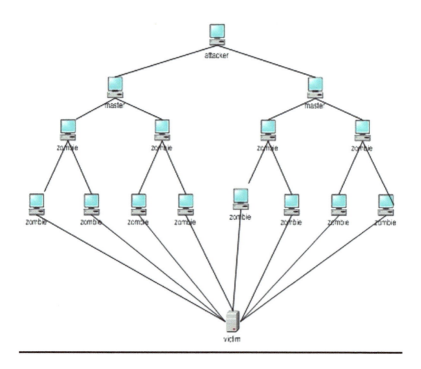

Figure 15: DDoS attack

2.5 Key Loggers

A keylogger is a type of surveillance software that has the capability to record every **keystroke** being made to a **log file**. A keylogger recorder can record **instant messages**, **e-mail**, and any information typed at any time using the **keyboard**. The log file created by the keylogger can then be sent to a specified receiver. Some keylogger **programs** will also record any e-mail addresses have been used and **Web site URLs** visited. Keyloggers, as a surveillance tool, are often used by employers to ensure employees use work computers for business purposes only. Unfortunately, keyloggers can also be embedded in **spyware** allowing your information to be transmitted to an unknown third party [25].

Windows Keylogger 5.04

Windows Keylogger 5.04 has some very good characteristics, thus it's being chosen from many others to be demonstrated. Some of the characteristics are recording the keystrokes in a log file and sending them to the attacker via email. It also destroys itself after a specific time, covering that way any tracks that may be traceable to the attacker. Even if the user suspects that something malicious is running on his computer, he will not be able to view keylogger in the CTRL-ALT-DEL-taskbar because it remains invisible [26].

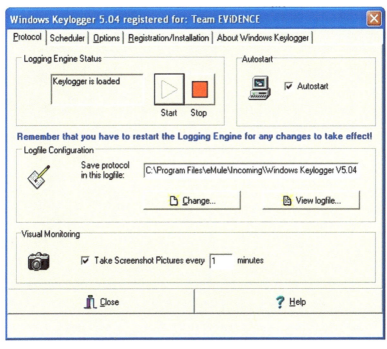

Figure 16: Keylogger 5.04 screenshot facilities

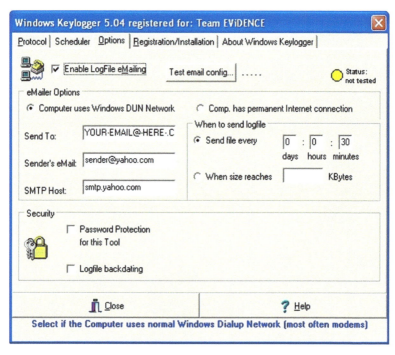

Figure 17: Keylogger 5.04 email facility

Perfect Keylogger

Having somebody behind your shoulder while you are using you Computer to deal with your bank accounts, isn't a good idea. This is what it may happened if an attacker manages to get through his victims computer and install Perfect keylogger **Figure 18**. Without realizing it the software will spy at the Computer, take screenshots of the desktop every few seconds or minutes, record all the keystroke activities and finally send the log files along with the screen shots at the attackers email address, even if the user realize that something suspicious is going on his computer, it won't be able to see it running in the Ctr+Alt+Del taskbar **Figure 19** [27].

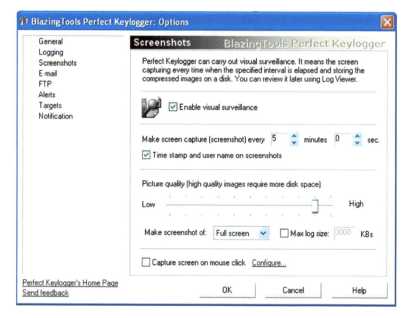

Figure 18: Softperfect keylogger Screenshots facility

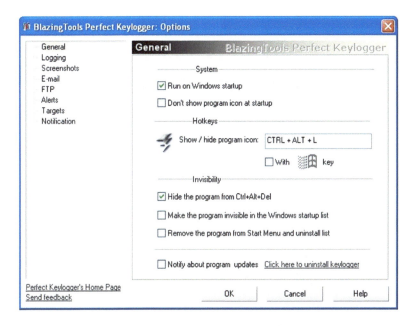

Figure 19: Softperfect keylogger hiding from
CTRL+ALT+DEL

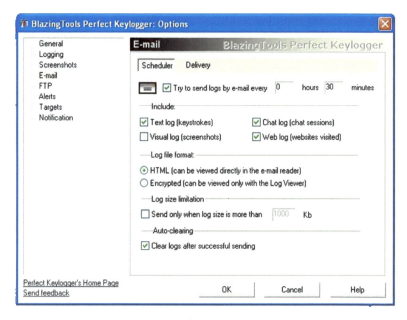

Figure 20: Softperfect keylogger email scheduler

Chapter 3

Analysis of hacking tools

3.1 Weaknesses and strengths of the various hacking tools

A variety of tools are out there and more of them are going to be created. For the purpose of this book only a few of them have been chosen and demonstrated. In this chapter weaknesses and strengths of those tools will be explained.

To begin with the approaching tool "SAM SPADE" it has been proved that it is a very useful tool to gain information about a target web site. Information about for example the company's competitors can be gathered and it can be found out when it has been created through the registration date of its particular web site, the server names of its company and its IP addresses to target. One very good site of this way of gathering information is that the victim doesn't have any idea of your activities because you are not requesting any details from the actual target server, the **whois** query is made at the registrants database, without living any tracks or any type of information, at the victims site.

Nmap ("Network Mapper") is a free open source utility for network exploration or security auditing. It was designed to rapidly scan large networks, although it works fine against single hosts. Nmap uses raw IP packets in novel ways to determine what hosts are available on the network, what services (application name and version) those hosts are offering, what operating systems (and OS versions) they are running, what type of packet filters/firewalls are in use, and dozens of other characteristics. Nmap runs on most types of computers and both console and graphical versions are available. Nmap is free and open source [9]. So that gives the ability to who ever finds any bugs and he is capable to fix them to do so. One of its best characteristics is the –sS option, in order to perform if not an invisible attack, at least the less visible to the target, in order not to have any after effects after the scan.

Netcat is a featured networking utility which reads and writes data across network connections, using the TCP/IP protocol. It is designed to be a reliable "back-end" tool that can be used directly or easily driven by other programs and scripts. At the same time, it is a feature-rich network debugging and exploration tool, since it can create almost any kind of connection you would need and has several interesting built-in capabilities [10]. One of its cons is that you will have to be familiar and like to work with command prompt in order to use it because it comes only with command line support and not with any type of GUI.

LANguard Network Scanner, here is where the nice GUI interfaces comes in place. LANguard gives as a Freeware security scanner for networks. It searches the network for hosts, shares and user names. Amongst many other functions it recognizes operating systems, as well as registry problems and tests password security. The scanner also provides comprehensive reports in HTML format on request [11]. The LANguard Network Scanner is a comprehensive and easy-to-use tool, but it doesn't support stealth signature like **nmap** and **netcat**, so using it may cause you being tracked if you don't know how to cover your tracks.

Softperfect Network Scanner is a free multi-threaded IP, NetBIOS and SNMP scanner with a modern interface and several advanced features. It is intended for both system administrators and users who are interested in computer security, which means that a normal user without administrative permissions can run it without any problems. The program scans for listening TCP ports and shows what types of resources are shared on a network. In addition, it allows you to mount shared resources as network drives, browse them using Windows Explorer [12]. Compared to LANguard, Softperfect gives as the option to use it with the command line and the ability to save our results to a file. Thought the GUI we can do a search for our external IP address if we are connected to the internet through a router. It is a very easy tool to use to gain the range of valid IP addresses along with their MAC address so if next time the host with the shared sources we found, changes its IP address we can track him using his MAC address. Not stealth signature option is one of the cons but quite important if you can't cover yourself and become visible to the other site.

Scanner	Windows	Unix	GUI	Command line	TCP	UDP	Stealth
Nmap	X	X	X	X	X	X	X
NetCat	X	X		X	X	X	X
LANguard	X		X		X	X	
Softperfect	X		X	X	X		

Figure 21: Network Scanners

3.2 Protection Methods against Hacking tools

@stake LC5 Countermeasures

To solve the problem we have with the **@stake LC5** tool we have to change the way that windows store our passwords through the registry, as demonstrated in **Figure 22**, so they will be much more secure.

By changing the registry value:

"My computer\HKEY_LOCAL_MACHINE\SYSTEM\Curre ntControlSet\Control\Lsa", and from there the value **"nolmhash"** to **"1"** the passwords are stored only in NT hash. That way they are much more secure than Lmhash [23].

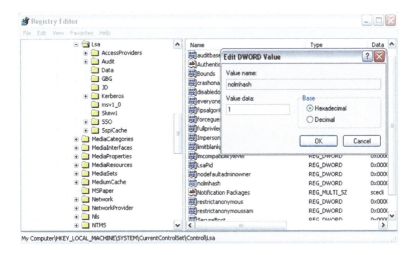

Figure 22: Registry editor

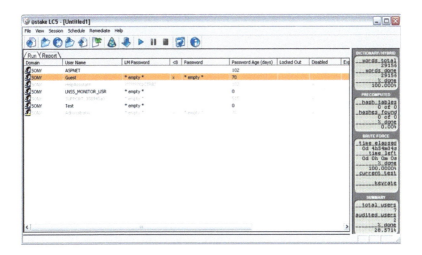

Figure 23: @stake LC5

As it can be seen in **Figure 23**, after changing the registry value, "nolmhash" to "1", our powerful tool **@stake LC5** did not manage to retrieve the same password that it did in 4 seconds, before the changes, even though it was left running for 04h 54m and 34s. That is because windows after the changes saves the passwords into NT hashes only, rather that saving the passwords in LM hashes and NT hashes.

3.3 Anti-Keylogger

Key loggers can be very disastrous if they are running without the user's knowledge, as they can monitor and log every single keystroke he/she presses, take print screens of the desktop every few seconds and finally email them to the attacker. Thus he will have all your usernames and passwords of your bank accounts and every other private information you have on the computer. Anti-key logger software such as the one demonstrated in **Figure 24**, is aware of the most common key loggers and can prevent them from running on the computers.

Another way, that banks use these days in order to prevent giving your passwords away, is to request the client to type in randomly chosen digits of his/her password. That way the attacker, even though he has a key logger on the bank customer computer, will retrieve useless digits [28].

Figure 24: Anti-Keylogger

3.4 CGI vulnerability Countermeasure

Security is a crucial issue when writing CGI programs, as the results of bad CGI codes in the demonstration with a vulnerable web site have been presented. Here some tips on how to write CGI programs which do not allow malicious users to abuse them can be viewed.

Here is a perl code example of a basic CGI with the common bug of no filtering mechanism to important user input:

```
------------------------------------------
#!/usr/bin/perl
use CGI qw/:standard/; # standard CGI
module
print header; # content-type header
$dir = "htmlfiles"; # directory where the
html files would be
$file = param("file"); # input from user
$fullpath = $dir . "/" . $file . ".html";
# create a full path
open(FILE, "<$fullpath"); # opens the
file, read-only mode
while () { print } # to print the
contents of the file
close(FILE); # close the file
# end of code
------------------------------------------
```

As we have experienced, the problem with this type of code is that a malicious user is able to read data that he/she shouldn't have access to. As seen, example of this is someone trying to read /etc/passwd.

There are two things that are required, which should be, but aren't, filtered in this program, to allow someone to read a file such as /etc/passwd.

1) Escape the directory that the open() statement would normally read in.
2) Escape the ".html" put at the end of the open()[29].

Here is our example of a URL that read the /etc/passwd on a machine running CGI code like the example CGI:

http://www.amicotelecom.com/call2pk/index.php?p =../../../../../../etc/passwd

3.5 DDoS attack Countermeasure

Distributed Denial of Service attack is a big problem, its something that system administrators have to be aware of and monitor all the time, in order for it not to manage to get through their systems. The main attacking method, as its being described in this book, is that the attacker uses his victim's computers to attack other computers and so on, and finally after he manages to enslave an acceptable large number of computers, he then orders them to attack at the same time a particular server. Once the DDos network is being built, the attacker can use it as many times he likes to perform attacks on any server. After an attack, the server can't handle the traffic, blocking all the legitimate clients that they wanted to use that server. Measures intended to make DDoS attacks impossible include simply making it hard for attackers to compromise enough machines, this could be possible if constantly people update their operating systems with any security patches are given by their vendors, installation of firewall, antivirus software and by making the servers more powerful so they can handle an ongoing attack and still be able to serve the legitimate clients.

3.6 Common security Measures

Along with any type of Operating System that comes into the disposal of the consumers, a number of security patches are following. This indirectly shows the endless battle that is undergoing between the hackers and the Operating System developers. Once the user have access to the internet, in order to protect itself it is essential to apply all the recommended patches that the OS Developer is creating. Also having installed security software such as Norton Internet Security, which contains both firewall and antivirus protection, is essential. For the network administrator's point of view, the server and all the hosts on the network must also apply those rules in order to avoid any possibly intrusions.

Conclusion

The more services a system provides to the outside world, the more vulnerable that system becomes. Companies nowadays are getting more and more internet oriented. People are relying on the power of the internet to sell their products, meet people, do their shopping, banking and so on. Inevitable the percentage of people that are using the internet is increasing every day, however most of them are unaware of the danger they are getting into, thus hackers are methodically, for a number of reasons, taking advantage of this technology burst that finding many people straggling with. Security measures that most home users don't know that even exist, from simple Operating System updates to the installation of antivirus software, are creating automatically easy targets for an attacker. In many cases companies do not offer enough training to their employees in order to protect their computers at work. In this continuous battle with the hackers, we have inherited with the technology revolution, we cannot afford to know less than the "enemy" to ... survive.

References

1. MAGAZINE, L., GO MOBILE, in LINUX MAGAZINE. 2005.
2. EC-Council, CERTIFIED ETHICAL HACKING. 2004.
3. Lewis, J., Wireless LAN Security. 2003.
4. **http://www.compuworks.com/home.php**. 2005.
5.
   http://research.pestpatrol.com/Lists/To pTenPestsByType.asp. 9 November 2005.
6. Atkins, S., Sam Spade 1.14. 1997-1999.
7. BBC, **http://news.bbc.co.uk/2/hi/americas/3657170. stm**. 14 September, 2004.
8. Bruce Schneier, C., Counterpane internet Security, inc, Hacking Exposed, ed. n. edition. 2001.
9. Hurnall, J. Nmap tutorial. 2003 [cited; Available from: **http://members.dodo.net.au/~ps2man/Nmap/ nmap.html**.
10. Shema Mike, J.B., Anti-Hacker Tool Kit. 2004.
11. **http://www.gfi.com/languard/**. 2003.
12.
    http://www.softperfect.com/products/n etworkscanner/. 12 January 2006.
13. Sutton, M., Hacking the Invisible Network. July 10, 2002.
14. Milner, M., **http://www.stumbler.net/readme/readme_0_4 _0.html**. 21 April 2004.

15. Jim Lockwood, S.L. Analysis of Benefits for Purchase of Network Protocol Analyzer. [cited; Available from: **http://www.peacefulpackers.com/it_solutions/t_index.htm**.

16. Combs, G. Ethereal. 2004 [cited; Available from: **http://www.ethereal.com/**.

17. Stein, L. CGI (Server) Scripts. 23 February 2003 [cited; Available from: **http://www.w3.org/Security/Faq/wwwsf4.html**.

18. admin@cgisecurity.com. Fingerprinting Port80 Attacks. 5 March 2002 [cited; Available from: **http://www.cgisecurity.com/papers/fingerprinting-2.html#intro**.

19. **http://cygwin.com/**. 2005.

20.   **http://packetstorm.linuxsecurity.com/Win/index2.html**. 31 January 2000.

21. Flam, D. Webcracker 4.0. 1999

22. @stake, I.S. LC5: The Password Auditing and Recovery. 18 May 2004 [cited; Available from: **http://www.atlguide2000.com/software/index.php?act=cat&cat=34**.

23. Kevin Rose, D.H. return of thebroken. 2004 [cited; Available from: **http://thebroken.org/**.

24. **www.whatis.com**. distributed denial-of-service attack. 2004 [cited; Available from: **http://searchsecurity.techtarget.com/sDefinition/0,sid14_gci557336,00.html**.

25. webopedia. keylogger. 2004 [cited; Available from: **http://www.webopedia.com/TERM/K/keylogger.html**.

26. Walter, C. 2002 [cited; Available from: **http://www.littlesister.de/**.

27.   software, B.t. Perfect Keylogger. 2004 [cited;
        Available from:
        http://www.blazingtools.com/bpk.html.
28.   Corporation, R. Anti-keylogger. 2005 [cited;
        Available from: **http://www.anti-
        keyloggers.com/**.
29.   [CommPort5@LucidX.com], s. Bug Classification
        Improper filtering of CGI parameters.   [cited;
        Available from:
        http://www.lucidx.com/5balgo1.html.

www.ingramcontent.com/pod-product-compliance
Lightning Source LLC
Chambersburg PA
CBHW041144050326
40689CB00001B/479